AGAINST VENICE

RÉGIS DEBRAY

AGAINST VENICE

Translated from the French by
John Howe

with an Afterword by
Régis Debray

PUSHKIN PRESS
LONDON

Copyright Editions Gallimard, 1995

Translation copyright © John Howe 2002

First published in 2002 by
Pushkin Press
71-75 Shelton Street,
London WC2H 9JQ

This edition first published in 2012

British Library Cataloguing in Publication Data:
A catalogue record for this book is available
from the British Library

ISBN 978 1 908968 88 3

Frontispiece: Régis Debray
By Jacques Sassier © Agence Opale, Paris

Set in 11 on 14 Monotype Baskerville by M Rules
Proudly printed and bound in Great Britain by TJ International
Padstow, Cornwall on Munken Premium White 90gsm

www.pushkinpress.com

AGAINST VENICE

UNTIL YOU HAVE LAID the ghost of Venice within you—repressed every posture, leaning, pretension, temptation or daydream capable of being described as "Venetian"—you will never be on level terms with the internal enemy. For that is where Flaubert's Homais[1] still clings on the eve of the third millennium, that is his Noah's Ark: the "city of marble and gold", the most vulgar resort frequented by people of taste (those whom works of art render blind and deaf to commonplace historical reality).

This is not a fixation of mine. Nor is it my fault—or yours—that Western history has set the family jewel at the top of the Italian boot, glittering obscenely and tenaciously in the fold of the groin. I mean to see the thing for what it is, without taking sides, without sourness, with the cold eye of a drunk: back on the bottle after five cures and ten placebos, but determined this time to get off it for good.

Let no one come and plague me later with allegations of resentment, vengeful passion, sour grapes. Of course I learned in class how and why to venerate this educational town, just as I mounted the podium to recite "*Homme libre, toujours tu chériras la mer*" and visited the Louvre to stand yawning in front of *The Marriage at Canaa* (so rashly appropriated from La Serenissima by Bonaparte). Like all schoolboys. But I have never identified closely with Venice, in the manner of those patriots who sometimes claim to be "sick for France". The most I can say is that I have suffered to see so many of my well-meaning contemporaries, myself included, shackled to that most essential of educational fairylands, that holy of holies of the pleasure principle. Perhaps a few rustic observations may help liberate two or three timid souls from all nostalgia for *vaporetti* and creaking jetties. Enable them to break with this collage, to deem the incident closed, to have done with the Obligation. I even toy with the irreverent idea of using the language of preventive medicine to influence coming generations . . . . Don't take Venice, a drug which is only pleasurable on the first "trip". Anyone might be led into it once, just to be like everyone else. But take a look into the nearest culture-boutique and see what the habit has done to your elders.

ODE TO JOY, *The Marriage at Canaa, Harmonies du soir*. It takes time to register the distinctive signs of facile work, time not for reflection but cross-checking. It isn't that I have any vocation to become a clinician of the glib, an acknowledged expert on paste and sham (life is too short after all). But with advancing age one sinks deeper, one starts to feel surrounded. And let's be serious; I am not talking about Millet's *Angelas*, Strauss waltzes or the *Élégies* of François Coppée,[2] poet of the humble.

For many years my body sniffed out imitation from a distance, without daring to draw nearer. Whenever a charming dinner-companion mentioned one of these test pieces in a favourable tone, it refolded its napkin and called for the bill. The head shrank from the scene of explanation, mused over the dots on the i's, dreamed of one day being rid of the shameful confusion between true and fake. Excuses were made. Little by little, however, the road signs ("give way to traffic from right") started to establish a code. One or two measures were taken, reluctantly. Just as, at fifty, some sort of dietary self-defence becomes necessary, to unload the bad fat from a thousand superfluous dinners, to carry on jogging or riding a bike, so the organism has eventually to face the need for dietary discipline in images and sounds, to carry on feeling through its own soul rather than the souls of others. To clear out all the occupants. Perhaps Beethoven, Veronese and Baudelaire should be seen as contra-indicated, like sugars and lipids. But to leave it at that would be to leave the job unfinished.

Internal obesity calls for more draconian treatment, an operation at source. For the character who admires bright vainglorious brocades, the contrived seesawing rhymes of *Les Fleurs du Mal* or Ludwig's humanitarian male voice choirs is, you can be sure, a "lover of Venice" *by nature*, the sort of person who is sent straight to seventh heaven by a pink Tiepolo ceiling.

You are going to stop me with the classic interjection: "but it's much more complicated than that". I have already been told, thanks: there are also the *Quartets*, the *Calvary* and the *Salons* or *Le Spleen de Paris*. It goes without saying that Beethoven's work is not exclusively emphatic; that the decorator who produced *The Triumph of Venice* and other heavy mundanities (low-fat painting, like 45% butter) sometimes seems aware that existence is not all feasting, rich velvet and heroic poses; and that Baudelaire the art critic and portraitist of modern life becomes the "perfect chemist", achieving in prose the poetry that a laboured, over-polished satanism denied him in verse (a counterfeit Titian, at his best when content to be a real Constantin Guys[3]). But in none of these three cases was the authentic predominant;

they are listed, homologated and confirmed by their respective fan clubs as a grandiloquent musician, a mundane painter and a poetic poseur. I do not deny that in some peripheral areas of Venice, like the zone to the north of the railway station, between the fuel storage depot and the Baia del Re, or the quarter at the other end of the island, to the east of the Arsenal (not the disused one preserved for show, the real one with the small working boatyards), round the Canale di San Pietro, the aesthete at dusk may at last feel himself to be in a strange place, cast into anonymity, lost in a desolate Chiricoesque[4] no man's land without the slightest hint of local colour. Not everything in the lagoon is nauseating, I admit, any more than in the complete works of Baudelaire.

On the spot, I have myself sometimes been seized with a sort of ambivalence, not knowing how to prise the nugget out of the surrounding matrix. I have sometimes dreamed not of death in Venice but of a thoroughly dead Venice, with all its overbearing domes, pinnacles and lantern-skylights fallen, and only the triangular pediments of the Scuola Grande di San Rocco left standing. Gesuati and Gesuiti, hump-backed bridges, tritons, lions and crocodiles: let them all slide into oblivion, provided this heart is left intact, with the ovoli on the ceilings and the canvases on the walls, from the *Annunciation* on the ground floor to the *Crucifixion* in the Sala dell'Albergo: the vital organs of Imagination Man will still be safe.

Nothing can better illustrate this perplexity than the central gallery of the Accademia, a long rectangular box that juxtaposes *Dinner at the House of Levi*, covering one entire wall, with, on the reverse of the opposite wall, *The Arrest of St Mark*. Veronese's *trompe-l'oeil* is so integrated into the architecture of the room, and beyond it the decorative spirit of the centre of Venice, that this great concoction, riotous colour without an atom of pain or a highlight of truth, seems not only framed but actually held up by columns and semicircular arches … after a while the bewildered eye starts to find these difficult to identify: are they part of the museum, or of the dwelling of the said Levi? Do they belong to the rococo surroundings or to an episode in holy history? Then, at the corner, you pivot on your heel and Tintoretto's uppercut mows you down without warning. So that, under the same washed-out zenithal light, a showbiz production rubs shoulders with a consignment to the abyss, a peep-show with a chasm, without any gradation. Like the simultaneous projection on a single split screen of Cecil B. DeMille on the right, Orson Welles on the left. But we shouldn't flatter ourselves. In the Venice that people concur in holding to be real (even if Welles did go there to shoot a single sequence of *Othello*, in black and white) the right side of the screen crushes the left. Baroque in stereo and Technicolor is what fills shelves, mouths and aircraft. That is the superproduction being considered here: Venice *orbi*, not *urbi*. But watch out. The trail of the jet set, who no longer trust cheap makeup, is recycled by every Tom, Dick and Harry in the form of a confidential this-is-all-I'm-telling-you. "You'll see," murmurs the tourist in his *trattoria*, furtively lowering his voice, "on this route, you won't see a single tourist." The alternative itineraries—all different, known to *absolutely nobody* else, avoiding the fatal Rialto-Doge's Palace-la Salute triangle—that the old connoisseur promises you if you are very good, like a lollipop to a griping brat, are the most attaching thing of all. And they are the last to lose their appeal. So listen: you will have to wrap up warm around the neck.

JUST AS THERE ARE different casts of mind, so there must be different types of visual sense, of touch or scent, as it were family differences. Perhaps our aversions are programmed at birth, our personal mythologies genetic. With age and experience simply making us aware of them (if sometimes still unaware enough to come clean). If so, it is only decent, before anything happens that might arouse animosity, to lay my cards naïvely on the table.

The theatre isn't really me. Nor golden hair, nor Rubens, nor Poussin either. What I am is cinema (whose inventor is called not Lumière or Edison but Il Tintoretto); burnish and mottling, Rembrandt and Caravaggio. I am as bored by symmetry, verticals and horizontals, the beauties of balance, as I am by people who find instead of seeking. I like it when time disturbs space, destabilises it, chops it through with diagonals and bleed lines. I prefer pride to vanity, existence to essence, the *Dies Irae* to the *Alleluia Chorus*, red wine to champagne and Rimbaud to Baudelaire. In a word, Naples is my scene, Venice isn't.

People call this little oddity of mine "populism" or even demagogy. I can accept the first label but not the second. And as nice people always arouse my liveliest antipathy I do my best, whatever the cost, to rub my brethren up the wrong way at least part of the time.

THE PLACE ITSELF, with its absence of greenery, its lack of relief, its shortage of sea views, might easily be thought suffocating. Not so: the visiting foreigner enjoys, in what many inhabitants experience as a prison (the young in particular see Mestre as the exit, a gateway to hope), a wholly new sensation of freedom. The visitor who arrives by train early in the morning and boards the No 1 *vaporetto* finds himself bobbing festively about in a dancing unreality. Life becomes less burdensome, there is a glorious insouciance, unexpected but quickly embraced; a euphoria that recalls something of childhood. The place has a well-known magic about it, a sorcery not explained by the grandeur of buildings that are not all that grand, or by boats put-putting picturesquely among the houses. If what you want is canoeing in the street or lakes instead of squares, you can find them in Amsterdam, Bangkok or Bruges. The secret of this wonder lies elsewhere: in the sudden joyousness of the game. Venice plays at being a town and we play at discovering it. Like urchins, like actors. With time for a time suspended, we abandon the seriousness of real life for the as-if of a charade of life. It's like going up in a balloon.

A straightforward museum-town would be as depressing as a holiday task. The palaces along the Grand Canal, which are not on display under glass, are not out-and-out Hollywood mockups, but neither are they real houses for living in. One might not be able to imagine living in them, but these pseudo-dwellings can be touched: they stand before us, but do not really exist. They are like solid reflections of their reflections in the water. No one peers down from the balconies; there are no signs of the domestic activity or random movement that can be seen anywhere else, the banging shutters, the concierges, the children, the housewives with shopping baskets; and at night only a loggia or two shows light, an occasional furtive shadowy movement. Just enough to make the story plausible, the décor almost believable. This city with its theatres, its opera house, its masked balls, is a theatre itself. And just as the week of Carnival is not parenthetical but allegorical in the universe of masquerades, La Fenice—a stage within a stage—is like the convex mirror in a Flemish painting, twisting and reflecting this theatre of shadow and water. Lounging on the terrace of the Al Teatro in the Gampo de la Fenice, seen and seeing, sipping a Campari, you are in the eye of the hurricane, the churning nucleus of the Venetian "action".

Venice is not so much a town as a representation of a town. In the Italian theatre the whole arrangement is pivoted not on the stage or the auditorium but on the footlights that separate them, for if they were on the same level there would be no spectacle. Similarly, what defines Venice is not Venice but the lagoon separating it from the profane, utilitarian, interested outside world, a patch of water that performs the function of a "semiotic break". Why does the Venice initiate advise postulants not to arrive by air? Because by being parachuted into the centre of the stage without first having taken the trouble to climb on to it, newcomers would be partly deprived—for luckily there is still some boat travel between Marco Polo airport and the urban heart—of the pleasure of clearing, of crossing the frontier (a moment that the more fanatical devotees transform into an act of mystical secession from the unutterable filth outside).

For centuries, arrival via Padua and embarkation at Fusina, five miles from the Piazza San Marco, for a leisurely crossing of the lagoon, symbolised (like a rite of passage) the change of physical and mental universe. Construction of the four-kilometre road and rail causeway between Mestre and the Piazzale Roma has simplified the crossing, but the fairly complicated procedure for leaving the car or bus in the parking area still maintains the intransitive essence through the trans-shipment, the change of vehicle *and of tempo*: a compulsory slowing down of vital rhythm has taken place; here we are, elsewhere and moving differently, on foot or like a cork on the water; no doubt about it, we have passed through from the other side of the mirror. Instead of whining about it as they would if someone used a hammer-drill during a Vivaldi concerto, devotees should rather praise the astuteness that has led to the nearest dry land being made so ugly, so vividly do the chemical plants of Marghera, the refineries, derricks and warehouses of Mestre, the tangles of petroleum and gas piping, the belching chimneys, by contrast underline the abyss that separates the fairy circle of aesthetic play, the *commedia dell'arte* we have just entered, from the sordid reality—so recently banished—of survival and the constraints of production: our modernity all befouled with infrastructures, barbarians and the oblivion of great art. Every acolyte's glance at the "hideous" skyline (which to me is like the view from a cell window: I stand right at the end of the Záttere and gaze at it, breathing deeply) renews the exorcism of the real world. And that, in sum, is the function socially reserved, from the outside, for the "fabulous marvel".

The stroke of genius here, in making the city of the Doges a permanent Living Theatre (and undoubtedly the best candidate for the title), is not the nth placement of an nth confection for the eye, but the chance we are given to have a turn at *being in the show*, where we can depersonalise in person, duplicate ourselves at will. The causeway built by Mussolini, and so aptly named Ponte della Libertà (freedom to escape from confinement for claustrophobes within; freedom to escape from themselves for hysterics without), enables the audience to come and mingle with the play being staged. *Anch'io sono attore.* In Rome, Naples or Milan we are forced to improvise; in most foreign towns we wander about haphazardly like characters in search of an author, in search of lines. But here the parts are already written, the moves chalked on the stage, and everyone can sidle into a libretto known by heart: in Naples we play an amateur walk-on part, but in Venice we are professionals. With invisible mask and domino, following the route laid down in a trail of arrows, everyone wanders from *campo* to *calle* to *campo* humming his little operetta tune, suitably disguised (it is during Carnival, when the pantomime is most apparent, that people act the least). The party is programmed, framed, rehearsed. In his blouse and red-banded straw hat the gondolier plays at serenading; the *facchino* at carrying the suitcases; the *cameriere* at serving us with scampi and *calamaretti* while whistling between his teeth; and we, between the Arsenal and the prisons, at being a spy on a mission, Casanova on the run, an intermediary, a world-weary dandy, a disgraced ambassador. Being a tourist, one can even play the tourist. Nothing is genuine. Two Capuchins in sandals pass before you, too obviously false; those lovers seem slightly too involved in saying goodbye behind a colonnade; and that phalanx of Japanese, lined up behind the flag, seem more martial than is reasonable. All those faceless extras hamming away to blend into the scenery, to "do Venice". Reboarding the train will be like taking off the greasepaint, putting the mufti back on, becoming Mr Everyman once again. The fact that in the meantime we can look at each other without dissolving into laughter should astonish no professional Thespian. One wonders whether the practising Venetians, the members of the local troupe, manage to keep cool heads. Probably, in view of the actor's paradox. But what does it matter whether the native Venetians believe in Venice or not? A *popolo minuto* swamped by the mass of recent arrivals on the boards, they know that the show must go on, that it earns their bread; in any case it is an old habit. The show is in the hall, and the hall is in the street. Look around you. Florid balconies, wrought-iron bridges, ensigns, chandeliers, stony scowls and pretty little faces skipping from trays in the shops; not a property is missing from the checklist. The curtain can go up on the latest Goldoni[5]. As an avant-garde touch, the producer has even placed a statue of the author in a corner of the stage, in the Campo San Bartolomeo.

Let us acknowledge that a work of art has the merit of transposition. The fine appearance does not trace reality but concentrates and recentres it, and through this shrinkage in the wash transfigures it. Here the representation is miniaturised, this snail-city not really being raw grandeur; the scenographic contraction mobilises the rule of the three unities (of place, time and action); and the change of scale adds to the "joke town" aspect, all that stucco and wrought iron, the conical chimneys, the jerry-built corbelling (with no humans behind it). The mock-up aspect (almost too perfect or finished) exalts an idealised urbanity, reduced to its essence, like a Platonic idea of a City, a self-sufficient microcosm. A toytown in which, in the middle distance of the as-if, there rejoices the destiny of all the splendours made by human hand, grandeur and decadence both. Every work of art places the real world in a reduced model and—since in art less is more—the recapitulatory ellipsis accentuates the effect of capture. The limited scale of the labyrinth, a surreal element, dramatises the oratorio, sharpens its point, fear of the dénouement; a dénouement postponed anew each day, with the complicity of those of us who are enrolled in the arrangement.

But the discomfort caused by the element of sham becomes more intense with every visit: this setting for subsidised life, absent from itself, exists only in and for the gaze of others. The meretricious does not support solitude well. Naples stripped of its visitors would still be itself, loud, fat and self-confident. But deprive Venice of its spectators, its extras, and it would decline and collapse in a week, its text dissolving, lost, haggard, like a great star forced to play nightly to an empty house.

VENICE has *style*. It might even be said that it has too many of them, seven or eight at least; but the disposition of the mosaic and the predominance of one material, white stone from Istria, make the composite of facades and architectures acceptable. Naples has something better: a tone. Here we have an exercise in composition; there, the imprint of a vital individuality, the unintended, irrepressible, vehement mark of a blind force. The Parthénopéenne[6] has no need to visit the hairdresser, or check its Rimmel in the glass every fifteen minutes like a rich lady with her compact after dinner. Naples depends on a temperament; Venice requires an education. Don't tell me that it is possible to like Anna Magnani in *The Golden Coach* and Alida Valli in *Senso* equally or at the same time, however inoculated you may be against the virus of antithesis. Whorish, fleshy, generous, insolent, with her car horns and bawled obscenities, the truculent southerner hurls herself on your neck, to your peril. A sensual hurricane with everything hanging out, sheets and underwear strung shamelessly across the street (in Venice the laundry dries in the courtyard, for decency's sake). She yells, sweats, stinks, screams, provokes. Venice is Nordic: a nice lady, to whom rumour attributes a list of notorious lovers, "still beautiful", cultivated, discreet, black lace, slim waist and fan. Undresses behind a screen. Has served many, but makes it a point of honour to be hard to get. Discreet wrinkles, a dim eye, sufferings contained and so forth (continued in the Harlequin collection).

NAPLES APPEALS to the photographer's strolling eye, Venice to the more applied organ of the painter. The reason seems to be that the first place is a chaos of traces, the second a harmony of lines. The raw just is (or isn't), for good; the finished recreates itself, recaptures itself with subtle touches. In the shadow of Vesuvius, photo-journalism is in its element;

the Magnum agency grew up there in the post-war period, from Cartier-Bresson to Riboud and Seymour in those days; Carlos Freire today. But in the lagoon, where all has become convention, even the best photo will have an air of pastiche: a failed painting or a museum piece. It is a place where Cartier-Bresson would have to swap his "single-shot rifle" for a double-barrelled pencil. A conscientious person who cares about the way things are done will draw the memorable corners of Venice from memory. In the *vicoli* of Naples, far from that cliché of a bay (which anyway vanishes as soon as one plunges into the metropolitan viscera), the opposite is true: the correspondence between sensation and sentient person is so exact that every shot snatched from the trash-heap gives off the unpredictable freshness of a miracle. No second thoughts or retouching are possible. The walker's gaze must try to be both subtle and wild: the paradise of the decisive moment, the photographer's promised land.

ANYTHING THAT TOUCHES on primitive myths is haunted by antithesis: what concern us here are the Water and Fire that lie behind mud and lava. Every raw material has its light of excellence, its alchemy; every bedrock its favourite sky. Venice is at its best after heavy summer rain, Naples in hot sunshine. I can't help it if in my heart of hearts fire generally extinguishes water.

THAT NAPLES should be so very "natural", in violent contrast to Venice the cultivated, where trees are proscribed (despite the belated invention of *giardini*, those timid Napoleonic violations of the artificiality imperative), is something that might mislead the ethnologist. The contrast is not between a "society without history" and a "society with a memory". Venice is a millennium old, Naples at least three times that, embodying an altogether different depth of time. A profundity that makes that egg full to bursting reverberate at length, like a vault or subterranean cavern which at every step reflects the echo of three or four cultures layered one on another. In the Via dei Tribunali, walls pissed against by mangy curs have a Greek base of carved white stone, restored here and there by the Romans with patches of red brick, and a roof level added later by a Spanish viceroy: twenty-five centuries in fifteen feet (and no sign from the cultural or tourist authorities to tell you so).

Naples, which does not see itself as the navel of the Mediterranean, gurgles like a stomach, our stomach. Brooding over the fire of several millennia, hiding in its entrails the gates of hell—to which people descended (Virgil *dixit*) through the Lake of Avernus, not far from the cavern at Cumae where the Sybil, the witch of the shades, frothed at the mouth. Just outside the gates of the city, in the Phlegethontal fields, there still well up vapours and sulphurous bubbles from the Solfatare, Vesuvius dozing uneasily with one eye open. A zone of panics and prodigies, of sacred horrors and great esoteric works, carved into the tuff[7] of Cyclopean epics and all the oldest Western dreams, Naples is a sun-drenched cellar between catacomb and mortuary chapel, geological honeycomb and paleolithic grotto. Modernity lounges at perfect ease in prehistory; farting, stuttering Hondas and Vespas pirouette over an African unchangingness of reflexes . . . generating a sort of *jeunesse patinée*, a time-polished youth to which no one would dare attribute an age: Persephone, Aeneas, Tiberius, the Anjous, Charles Quint, Garibaldi, Berlusconi . . . .

Vicissitudes have furrowed Venice's brow, but each of Vico's *ricorsi* has sanded smooth the face of Naples, as if with every spiral of time its vitality shone forth anew. In that politically destitute metropolis, fleeced by Rome (Stendhal said that "Naples is the only capital in Italy"), time weighs lightly and the very idea of decadence is hilarious.

Alas, there is only one Venice; but there will always be a Naples after (or rather on top of) Naples.

THE ISLAND CITY with its little finger genteelly stuck out, used as a drawing room by the whole planet, is a place where "people of quality" display common behaviour. While in the volcano town, shrieking with vulgarity, the common people project an air of distinction.

This does not prevent the lagoon from being ten times more frequented by tourists than Posilippo. The ones who do cross Naples scuttle through with lowered eyes, petrified of *scippo*, of pickpockets and bag-snatchers, heading as quickly as possible for that direst of school impositions, Pompeii. The popular town repels the populace, the snobbish one attracts it. An overwhelming majority for the adulterated and dressed-up. As usual.

IT'S SIMPLE, and magical. Naples is not an art gallery town for the simple reason that images are still alive there. Dolls, statuettes, puppets, plaster crib figures, Pulcinelli in smocks and black masks sacralise the frivolous, while "serious" painting and sculpture humanise the sacred. Image is omnipresent: over grocery stalls, above doorways, presiding over butchers' counters and displays, hanging from the ceilings of shops or placed in votive niches, behind grilles or not, overlooking the street. Dead effigies— the ones that no longer work against the evil eye— are deported to the museum of Graeco-Roman antiquities. Anyone can be on friendly terms with the others, the ones that still have souls; can dress them up, touch them for luck, caress them. Midway between talismans and reliquaries, they serve to wheedle the shades, domesticate the Void. Through them, every Neapolitan can negotiate small favours with the dead, striking innumerable Camorra-style deals: "I light a taper to you; you see me all right". Protection in exchange for deference: the fundamental pact. At the entrance to the Pompeii motorway, in the middle of an industrial wasteland, a baroque statue of San Gennaro stands upright, alone, holding back the streams of lava with an imperiously raised arm.

In Naples the rude childhood of the Image is naïvely exhibited; Venice, where curators, dealers and conservationists frame it and put it under glass, looks after its funeral rites.

> *I would never be lost*
> *For all the world's beauty*
> *But for a nothing in particular*
> *That cropped up by chance,*

St John of the Cross said. But there are places where you can be lost among myriad prettinesses without running the slightest risk.

NAPLES HAS a cheerful skeleton, with merrily winking eye-sockets. Venice fades the flesh, the honeymoon temple hastens the end of love. The comedian of the South invites the dead to the ball (a noisy, vulgar affair); the golden-haired Venus chills to the bone with the loom of shadow and death-rites. Is it the odour of mildew? The gloomy green of the canals? Charon's sooty barges, the crossings of the Styx by *traghetto*, the hundred small daily separations, the foundering palaces oozing water through every cranny? The coffin-like gondolas?

It is a little surprising that the newer town should distance itself from its dead by expelling them to the fortified island of San Michele, hiding the Reaper behind curtains of pinkish brick, while the old one parades all its tibias, exposes its death's heads to the four winds, sticks them on bollards, shovels them into unceremonious piles. Wherever you walk in Naples you are treading on an ossuary. Souls in purgatory behind their scarlet night-lights, the flayed in the San Severo chapel, the recumbent figure of Sammartino under his veil of marble, crypts converted into common graves: every crossroads reminds us of the universal terminus. Why should it be that Venice, sweet seaweed and wet sour wood, smells of necropolis, while the funerary Naples crackles with health? If I had to risk an answer I would say that Neapolitan idolatry, combining worship of images with worship of the dead—which used to be the prime function of the gaze—places bodies in an affectionate and gentle communication with their shades. Pleasure, an abundance of forms, tender magic, make the cadaver supple, overlay the death's head grin with a smile, fuse Eros and Thanatos. Hence the reversal of roles: the Neapolitan display of the corpse stimulates pleasure; the Venetian banquet has a taste of ashes. As if the expedient of easing the ugly brute out of the visual field in a short-term, short-life conservation reflex served against all expectation to advance the cause of nihilism.

IT IS POSSIBLE to weep hot and bitter tears in Naples, city of extravagances, for the same reason that hearty laughter is normal there; people do not sob in Venice, city of autumn, city of evening, for the same reason that Venetian gaiety must content itself with a thin smile. It is a polite place, where people get depressed but stop short of suicide.

COMPARED TO that swarming heap of live coral, nestled in its bay and exuding pathos from every pore, Venice cuts the figure of a carcass, an empty shell: not physically depopulated but spiritually dried out, dead to all magic (except through misuse of language). No doubt an aesthetic curettage of this sort was needed before it could accede to the status of "Pearl of the West", "Heritage of Humanity" and "Sanctuary of Beauty".

Basilica is a somewhat misleading term: despite the neo-Gothic ugliness of its facade, the Neapolitan Duomo (in which the skull of St Januarius is preserved along with vials of his blood) is a place of worship; while San Marco, despite the high masses celebrated there, is now just a place of culture where neglected altar-pieces grow old as curiosities. You can buy a ticket to stand in line during the service, along the Pala d'Oro, behind the choir (a bit like the great gallery in the Louvre, where no miraculous cures have ever been reported). But Venice only has churches; in Naples there is religion. Travelling from the Campania to the Veneto is a regression from African animism to cultural animation; a passage from Fang ancestor carvings, which protect against death and sickness, to negro effigies of the sort found in vestibules, lounging torch-bearers with white turban and plume. A lowering of intensity.

In Venice, a mirage *from which the sacred has fled*, you could find yourself believing that twelfth-century reliquaries and chalices were made for ornament. In Naples you get Beauty as a bonus; as before the birth of Art, as with the very finest works, which are the ones that have not been made on purpose.

THE RATHER PLEBIAN EXHIBITION mounted by Ernest Pignon-Ernest in Spaccanapoli in the late nineteen-eighties would have seemed profanatory in the City of the Doges: the placement of some five hundred drawings printed on paper, fly-posted straight on to the battered walls at pavement height, in the middle of the market quarter among Fiat 500s and children's games of hopscotch. Black and white posters with rough edges, unheralded, with nothing to say "Attention: art". A self-erasing, self-effacing labour, done for the pleasure of it. In Venice, where nothing is created and nothing gets lost, it would have had to be made to pay. The information department would have made a poster of the fly-posting, someone would have framed and gilded these fugitive marks; a conscientious arts commissar would have summoned critics and cameras, transatlantic foundations would have been solicited, and the work made the subject of seminars, catalogued, introduced, auctioned and judged. Everything would have been put back in order. But in the aesthetically offhand city of Naples a lofty but benevolent cheeriness, combined with dust and rain, gnawed the drawings away bit by bit; a few were appropriated in neighbourly fashion by interested parties and now hang on dining room walls, relics of the haphazard. Pasted up at night, these dead Christs, these Salomes and Mary Magdalenes, looked as if they had not been placed on or over the walls but emerged from, welled out of the stone. What was disturbing in this paradoxical encounter was the way the technical virtuosity of the drawing, the perfection of line, turned into a prehistoric nonchalance of form reminiscent of the wall art found in Aurignacian caves, where the unframed "picture" borrows and exploits the slightest unevennesses in the rock and the location counts more than the figure. Like the anonymous aurochs, vulvas or horses of the Magdalenian period, these Caravaggios and Michelangelos give the impression of extracting themselves from the walls, like living forms asleep in the rock, flowing out as if inadvertently on to the surface. Not works of art or precious objects, but the excrescences or stigmata of an invisible thrust of time, that the artist might merely have traced on the wall to make it visible to the passer-by. In the same way, present-day Inuits still carve ivory to extract the reindeer which palpitates in silence within the raw material.

This trust placed in natural light, in exterior space and the shifting viewpoint of the passer-by, did not just have the gift of "putting art back into life". It was no longer art, but a little more than life: verging on the in-between, the site of long-forgotten births of the Image itself. Everything indicates that in the age of flint and haematite a wall of rock was not an inert, neutral, opaque and meaningless base, like a canvas stretched over a frame, but a living interface where spirits and humans might meet: what was beyond (or in front of) appearances, invisible to our poor retinas imprisoned by surfaces. So that the sweating walls and black lava lining the alleys of Spaccanapoli became doors half-open for a moment on the Night and the Terrible, on a limbo from which emerged like accusing ghosts these white torsos, these twisted mouths, these knotted cadaverous arms; resumed in the twinkling of an eye their lost status as frontiers between two worlds: life and death. Like so many exhortations to risk a round trip.

THERE IS an illustrious photo of Lenin on a terrace in Capri, playing chess under Gorky's roguish eye. This laid-back holiday scene used to upset me in the old days. Revisiting Naples, that scene seems appropriate to the hint of something dangerous that crouches in that misleadingly idyllic-looking shadow-bordered bay: volcanoes, chthonian powers, eronic sacrifices, Caliguloid mysteries and excesses of every sort. How much more than comic, how *painful*, would have been a shot of Lenin lounging on the Rialto, Mao smoking a cigarette in front of the Bridge of Sighs, Che sprawled in a gondola. Those monochromes, not so much incongruous as unthinkable (except as Erró-style pop collages), would cause a short-circuit. Not because that conservatory so beloved of conservatives is associated by us with Viscontian demi-tints, with the great sepia-coloured game of the *fin de siècle*. The name alone serves as a recognised emblem to the *nouveaux riches* who come there to rub some gilt off the escutcheon and give it a bit of patina (not knowing, perhaps, that the socialists have a strong local following or that Visconti himself had communist leanings . . .). But because going to Venice is a discouragement: abdication from Utopia, renunciation of adolescence. It is the one place in Europe that best verifies the observation:

"The tourist is a person who, unable to change the world, changes his location within it".

All hopes shipwrecked long ago, all values liquefied into a weary Donjuanesque shambles, an old Prince of the left came to hang about and dream there, toying with the idea of acquiring a small palace on the Giudecca.

In a place that is silted up, failure may mean no more than running aground. Unless saved by luck and notoriety, every reprobate, every ageing nobody is confronted with private disasters and thus with this small challenge: to hold out as long as possible, to resist the Venetian pied-à-terre. *Vedi Napoli e poi muori?* All right. But if you want to see Venice, die first.

Cynics adore Venice. So do nihilists. Retired rakes and Casanovas relish the odour of slime. We should hang on to our surviving fragments of naïvety. It is such a fragile virtue.

THERE IS a hierarchy in despair. Defeated, rejected by the French, de Gaulle went to Connemara for some fresh air. Who could possibly imagine him "in the evening of his life" walking briskly into the breeze on the beach of the Lido, stick in hand and black raincoat over his arm? In Venice you aren't in exile; you are stroking yourself.

Maintain quality control. If your despair seems to be taking a Venetian turn, chuck cold water over it. Take it to Ireland by force.

EUROPES IN DECLINE follow one after another, but they are not alike. 1890 Vienna produced thinkers; 1990 Venice, introverts. This rest-house coddles our melancholy, the last stage before sloth. And of all our feelings, this is the one most inclined to see itself as a meditation. For one quicksilver Morand, for one mandolin *pizzicato* from Fauré, how many boating songs are there, how many serenades and other pieces of gondolier kitsch (a word, incidentally, that seems to come from the wrong country)?

History teaches us that merely falling asleep is not sufficient to forge the key to our dreams.

THE VENETIAN is to tragic feeling what the Sulpicien[8] is to religious art.

VENICE HAS an unbeatable address book. It is undoubtedly of all towns in the world the one with the heaviest share of incorporated social capital, proportionately more than Paris; the town where the number of clichés per square metre surpasses the levels prevailing in comparable sites (Florence, Rome,

Athens). From Commynes to the Princesse des Ursins, Petrarch to Anna de Noailles, the most unfettered spirits have come here to feed their souls—or rather to frame themselves in the fretted plasterwork— leaving the most "pathetic" *adieus*, the most "sublime" incantations, ringing in our ears to this day. With the result that this animated object, which has more souls than it should, is not just a "town filled with art" like the others. It is Art *made* Town: an Object better than rare, absolute, unreproduceable, vaporising the very idea of mass production and the multiple. The perfect original. This hyperbolic singularity (which anyone can appropriate merely by paying tribute to travel agents and local *ciceroni*) makes its explorer a unique being in his turn, an exceptional accomplice, through ambulatory or contemplative contagion. Being at ease there, and chatting about it, confers great status. Self-promotion. The Rotary emerges affiliated to the Jockey Club. Big jump guaranteed.

Voltaire sniffed out the catch. Threadbare or rolling in money, but on foot, along the Grand Canal, "we are all kings". All being milorded by an invisible lackey. Like the six poor unknowns in Venice for the carnival whom Candide, dining at their table, discovered all to be Serene Highnesses in exile. Those Turco-Gothico-Renaissance casements peering snootily down at us, those corner balconies at the Danieli, the terraces of the Gritti and the Hotel d'Angleterre, upstage us with absolute invincibility. They have an *aura*, a word Walter Benjamin translated as "the unique phenomenon of a distance, however close it may be". What is the distance that appears to us through these blind arcades and trefoils of stone, and that would not appear anywhere else? Shadows with names like Musset, Sand, Stendhal, Balzac, Wagner, Thomas Mann, Byron, Rilke, Hemingway and the rest. Spectres that glide towards us in an intimidating cortège, shining in the dark, passing through walls. Demigods who have come through the mirror, emerged from a washed-out silt-bed of colour prints and ritornels, the most enviable file of image-makers and wordsmiths that any anthology could list. The ultimate distinguished city makes the unknown individual distinguished, through its ability (periodically reactivated with the topping-up shots of books, articles, films and reproductions) to co-opt him into the circle of dead poets. More than any work of art, which is portable and can change owners, this real-estate patrimony thus fulfils its role as the federator of an elite cutting across frontiers and centuries, the turntable of a brotherhood of out-of-the-ordinary connoisseurs with armorial quarterings going back to the Crusades: the "lovers of Venice". We know that animism attributes to a fetish those qualities of the tribe that the tribe has deposited in it. Let us not lend this pianoforte the talent of its players. When we chant these spells, it is to our own culture, our own coteries, that we are paying tribute: to our own personal and exclusive capacity for rapture.

The definition of a work of art, as Michel Melot has shown so well in the case of engraving and sculpture, is haunted by problems of quantity (limiting the number of proofs, the scarcity of buyers, marks of uniqueness on the object). Have we really considered all that a cultural holy communion implies in terms of excommunication? Everyone loves Venice in order to be different from everyone else. Worrying, though, are the inauthenticity, the sad plagiarism, the second-hand aspect of the writings and conversations these days devoted to this common denominator of smart people, whose most unarguable claim to usefulness seems to be that it vaccinates the upper classes against the epidemic of commonness and vulgarity. The price of entry: an obligatory ecstatic posture and flood of epithets. But these are just pretexts, a matter of fixing the appointment. People swagger, they go for the top. Just as the word "snob", which may be derived from "*sine nobilitate*", in any case refers to the absence of nobility in commoners wearing borrowed plumes, so the aesthetic of cruising dancing-pumps seems to embody the feelings of people who are anaesthetised to art, but determined to drive crass hobnailed boots out of a sanctuary they long to render exclusive. Excluded, themselves, from the studios where the eye of tomorrow is being developed, guardians of the temple who want to be "in the loop" do their utmost to keep out the philistines, meaning everyone else. Each poses as the key member of an unfathomable conspiracy, the sole holder of the true password.

The real joke of this retrograde social climbing is in the huge numbers of postulants, underlining the vulgar *arrivisme* of the thing with the massive unanimity of denial. Doubtless it entered the realms of utter ridicule back in the sixties, with the industrialisation of travel, charter flights, hippies, rock concerts and the "leisure civilisation". The sight of two broke, bare-chested trippers with "structuralist beards", gulping grappa out of the bottle, was enough to send Paul Morand into the deep depression described in the closing passage of his post-1968 work *Venises*. Hardly surprising: how would you like being harassed by rubbish in the supreme crypt itself, when as early as 1933 you had asserted that "At this moment all countries, except our own, are exterminating their vermin"? For myself, in the middle nineteen-nineties, I cannot claim such a beleaguered-aristocrat, Marquis de Cuevas level of disgust and horror, but I can admit the irresistible hilarity inspired by a spectacle that has become routine during Easter or Ascension weekend: a hundred thousand anaesthetised aesthetes in tee-shirts, crammed into an area the size of a handkerchief, ankle deep in greasy food wrappers and beer cans, hunting in packs for the crucial tiny difference in the same shot through the viewfinder of the same Japanese camera. "O thou most irreplaceable of beings!" Number has overtaken quality: an object-lesson in the inversion of values by practices. Each *campo* ladles out, in bulk, its minestrone of dainties, its *polenta* of the exquisite. The unique stick together. The hallmark of Venice, this communism of egos, is a turnaround worthy of Goldoni: mass individualism hoist by its own petard.

VISITING THE "sanctuaries of art" is usually rather like going to a private view: a glance at whatever is hanging on the wall between handshakes and greetings. The canvases fill the gaps in the conversation. The benefit is not so much aesthetic as sociological. What enraptures is the jostling; not the thing itself, but the clamour around it.

IN NAPLES nobody would dream of asking you with whom, or in what hotel, you are staying: it is a matter of indifference. In Venice there is no escape: Gritti? Danieli? Duc de C's palazzo? M's apartment? (Total consternation if the answer is "Youth hostel" or "University dormitory"). In the theatre—unlike the anonymous auditorium of a cinema—the distance of a seat from the stage has a social, almost moral significance. You are never in the second row of the stalls, or the upper balcony, merely by chance.

A DOUBLE-PAGE spread in a major magazine, April 1995: the usual slipshod selection of platitudes on la Serenissima by a "prestigious writer", under the title: "Mitterrand the Venetian". Commonplace from beginning to end: Trattoria Antonella, city as woman, pleasure and decline, angel of la Salute, splendours of art, eternal Opera, lesson of beauty, Musset, Barrès. Academic ideas for an academic town, suburbs snorting with contempt. All is well.

Why does Venice turn the heads of French academicians? Two out of three of them go there to drink it all in, noisily. As if it were part of the job. Concession by the department? Tradition? Privilege?

43

"Perhaps," Franca Baratto, patrician and rebel, tells me over lunch at the Vini da Gigio in San Felice. "But we have Rezvani in the house too. Zoran Music, Boucourechliev. And remember Luigi Nono." And the permanent exception of Tintoretto (a subject on which Rezvani meditated), which tramples the rule underfoot.

I tip my hat to the malicious smile of my friend, who is a Venetian and communist of impeccable lineage; to the wisdom of old establishments, their artistry in having the last word. Venice brings out its great solitaries in much the same way that the French Church produced its two resistance-connected cardinals in the summer of 1944.

The venice idiot is not the Venetian born and bred (who, even when he does not actually earn his bread from it, tolerates the art farce with admirable self-restraint, although it costs him dear in exorbitant rents and food prices). He is the foreign noble who is obviously mad on Venice, mad from nobility and by nature, since the passion for Venice has become the statutory characteristic of Verdurins aspiring to be Guermantes, and who will be tough-minded enough to sneer at the almost Sicilian superstition of hysterical candle-carriers at the feast of San

Gennaro. But he will never ignore a collection box or fail to join the queue for the Correr or the palazzo Grassi. A devotee without knowing it, he has swapped processions for queues. The true devotee goes to Venice once a year, with somewhat less difficulty than his ancestor had in making the pilgrimage to Santiago de Compostela. Our senior manager loiters in front of the Accademia because he has espoused that most socially uplifting of all the current credulities: the religion of art. An espousal of convenience, of convention. The creed that pervades the atmosphere has coloured the attitudes of our earnest museum-freak through a sceptical and resigned sort of osmosis. For the air of today is to the time of Ruskin, Proust and Malraux what the Church Triumphant was to the struggling Church of apostolic times. High priests, professors of Beauty and revelations are only accessible to the believer of the year 2000 through the *Guide bleu*, folding maps, special issues of magazines, colour supplements. For the eucharists of the Beautiful are no longer bestowed and received; they have to be *procured*. In 1900, Proust had finished translating the Amiens Bible line by line before taking the train for his Mecca, accompanied by his mother. A snapshot shows him there in profile, sitting in a wicker chair overlooking the Adriatic, his moustache and undersized bowler hat strongly suggesting Charlie Chaplin.

Proust had been set on the trail of the church of the Schiavoni in imagination simply by reading Ruskin's chapter on Carpaccio. The would-be Proustian of a century later is guided there by courtesy of Michelin tyres, not by a rebound copy of Ruskin's *The Stones of Venice*, subtitled "Introductory chapters and local indices for the use of travellers while staying in Venice and Verona". So it is not the same St Jerome who appears to the dedicated predella enthusiast, at the end of the same canal and the same childish daydreams, overlooking the "endless trembling and shimmering of the lagoon". And there is an ever-growing risk of mistaking commentaries on commentaries for feelings.

The magnetic field of "beauty deposits" has lost in intensity what it has gained in extent. The authorised references are piled so high that it is becoming increasingly difficult to find one's way through the archive. Proust's Venice had been sculpted by thirty years of reading, and by visions based on a painting by Titian (which had given him an incorrect idea of the relative positions of the lagoon and the piazza San Marco, soon corrected on the spot). Ours has not been truly desired, nor conquered through stern internal struggle against ten childhood fantasies, a hundred engravings and a thousand material difficulties, like a rare, long-coveted gift guaranteed to retain its magical aspects. It is the rushed purchase of a man in a hurry going for the easy option: a dozen roses in cellophane, snatched in passing for Mothers' Day. To keep everything correct.

The aborted journey at the end of *Swann's Way* was an imaginative success for Proust. All we have to do is get to the airport in time to catch the plane, follow the plan closely, find our reserved hotel room and leave three days later with the slightly sheepish impression that we have missed our objective, that the real thing has somehow escaped us. For all we have seen is the visible Venice, down-at-heel palaces, fat people walking about, not "the city of marble and gold highlighted with jasper and paved with emerald"; not "these amethyst rocks like a reef in the Indian Ocean"; not "men as majestic and terrible as the sea, bronze armour gleaming through the folds of their blood-coloured cloaks" who at 45, rue de Courcelles so raised the temperature of Ruskin's young reader that his doctor forbade him to make any travel plans.

For centuries Venice was seen as Oriental, as an enigma. Perhaps now it has become a fabulous

Occident for young Japanese newlyweds. While remaining for the average European a bazaar of cut-price sensation and export-reject elegance.

THERE ARE NO VISIONS in Venice any more, just confirmations. Nature imitating art? These constructions in stone are just its residue. Not that this town is an absence, as Sartre imagined it one day while gazing from his hotel window, a sort of seasickness, an unbearable spinning void. "Venice is that place where I am not." What I am more inclined to say, alas, is that it is that place where others have always gone before me, forcing me to follow in their footsteps wherever I go. Constructed more by writers than masons, designed more by painters than architects, made more of words than bricks, it is a fabric woven of reminiscences, not an individual hallucination but an effect of collective belief. A "relational paradigm", socialised to the core, that serves better than any other human concretion to verify the well-established rule, more pertinent to artistic than scientific matters, that the discourse on a thing is an integral part of that thing. The Venetian commonplace does not exist in itself—no more than the *Mona Lisa*—and its own specific consistency will continue to fade.

The "marvel" is not vouchsafed to us in the candour of an early-morning vision, like the Virgin appearing in the depths of a cave to transform the life of an illiterate Bernadette. Venice is first and foremost a literary and pictorial memory. The "vision" comes as a response to centuries of jottings and markings; what we see is the latest link in an endless chain of small equivalences, more or less compulsory thoughts, more or less exact translations. The mutation of things into signs, sharpened by the strangeness of the "street with the best houses in the world" (as Commynes described the Grand Canal), by the bizarre juxtaposition of floating palaces and ornate pirogues.

We ourselves are afloat on a raft of references, every glimpse of the landscape releasing, like a conditioned reflex, this or that association with some paragraph, picture or sequence.

In a word, there can be no enchantment more studied, no dawn more worn and rumpled, than on this memorial lagoon.

"VENICE THE RED", Musset's poem called it. Yes: red as a Légion d'honneur. Let's protect our ribbons, let's leave the bemedalled their privacy, to celebrate themselves together by toasting the Chinese at the

Florian[9] and admiring the "dancing pumps gliding over the soft water"; let them spray each other with citations, let them make their proprietorial rounds. While we slope off to Hong Kong or San Diego, bracing crudities still untouched by metaphor, places that Musset, Byron, D'Annunzio and Henri de Régnier had the decency never to visit. Because, really, the most vexing thing about this palimpsest of multicoloured marble is the way it prevents us from improvising. The *veduta* only leaves us the choice between recitation and graffiti. Culture and *inculture*. Only the third term is worthwhile.

IN NAPLES, where the stone angels often have grave expressions (as they should), I become an idolater again. Like a child, a contemporary of Homer, a mediaeval pilgrim. All ready to race forward and snuggle into the arms of vermilion Virgins and dull-silver saints, to hide beneath their emerald- and diamond-encrusted garments. When I am there I believe in the Mother image. For the simple reason that the Neapolitans believe in it themselves, and in votive offerings, talismans, amulets. They stamp their feet to St Januarius, before the reliquary with the vial of black blood. They cross themselves on every occasion, light candles, call on the small icons dotted about the streets in their niches (there is even a colour print of Marilyn as the Virgin Mary: I am told that a mysterious hand used to replace the violets and pansies on the edge of her niche at a crossroads).

By contrast the sculptured porches, the friezes, cornices, columns and figures of Venice would make me an iconoclast, like a Huguenot under the Counter-reformation, if the votive images there were still recruiting true believers. Here the baroque is too much because it is only there (or only still there) for the swank. The carved angels of la Salute or San Moisè are not saving anyone. The Venetians of today apparently expect nothing of them. They take no notice of guardian angels or miraculous images, their faith has gone, they want cash machines. In San Giorgio or the Schiavoni, I see no more candles, lilies and people at prayer than in the boxes at La Fenice or in the first, Byzantine rooms of the Accademia. Theatre-churches, museum-churches without God or believers, appropriate in this Republic without a people. Once the sacred image has been degraded into a work of art, magical expectations die down and fade into absurd, petty simonies. Under each *Nativity* or *Deposition from the Cross*, in the side aisles or above the altar, there is a metal box with a slot for your two-hundred-lire coin, to switch on the thirty-watt bulb for a minute. Unable to charge for entry, the verger can at least make you pay for liturgical contemplation. In the mini-Babylon of the cultured, a glance at the angels may no longer bring salvation, but that does not prevent it from being lucrative.

ONLY SOMEONE as inflexible as André Breton, a man who made no allowances, could refuse on principle to set foot in the City of the Doges. It would have involved too much compromise. Should we regret the inventions, the celebrations, the magic, that might have been made by the brains and hands of those who instead obtained them, for the sake of convenience, from specialised establishments? That is the meaning of the economical attitude shown by the surrealists who, strengthened by their continence in Venetian matters, had all the more time to sublimate at home, to our greater pleasure and benefit.

THE VENICE IDIOT, to give the devil his due, knows how to kill two birds with one stone: he goes in for both tourism and holidays, activities that are normally dissociated. The tourist forgets himself in the discovery of the wider world; the holidaymaker intends to forget his world and rediscover himself.

The summer vacationer chooses regression by going to the beach and delivering his skin in pagan fashion to the sun and the water. By donning shorts the citizen casts aside the ageing man he normally inhabits, magically annulling briefcase, office-politics minuet and endless scheming. He denies and thrusts away the ordinary components of his daily existence. A bathing costume for a dip in the fountain of youth: a somewhat disingenuous naturalism, no doubt, but disarming, because he is laying down the weapons of his culture. The cultural tourist by contrast becomes even more serious than usual, and equips himself with guidebooks, maps and navigational instruments before plunging methodically into the unknown: Touraine, Tuscany or the Zambezi. Venice, though, maximises the return on the cost of the journey by combining both advantages.

I can feel, almost, the thrills of a Stanley in the Congo while hacking, nose in *Guide bleu*, through the jungle of *rii* and *sottoporteghi* (vizored helmets have a shape strangely reminiscent of solar topees): a serious gent, earnestly buckling down to some work. But in the very act of playing the studious explorer, the creature of a learned discipline, I can be gambolling in carefree fashion, being young again, withdrawing into my navel and shelving my "adult responsibilities". In this strongbox of time, the banker shuts himself away to forget the economy, the politician politics, the office worker his boss. The lagoon offers both memory and forgetfulness, rootedness and nomadism; immersing us in past worlds while obliterating today's hinterlands.

The holidaymaker's beach turns its back on the country: a single low trick that justifies its entire cost. Venice too keeps its environment at a distance on both seaward and landward sides. In this island outside the world, this pond of history without geographical borders, what visitor ever thinks or cares about Padua, Austria, Trieste or Dalmatia (which nevertheless give it its depth, its setting and ventilation, *bora* and *scirocco*)? Venice for us is a littoral without hinterland, where Friuli is a thousand miles from our thoughts, as far as the Club Med at cap Skirling from the forests of Casamance that surround it. As a result there is no need to go as far as the Lido, a place as impersonal and macadamised as Le Touquet-Plage, to get some of the essence of bathing. The kiosk at the Ca'd'Oro is all I need to throw aside mentally my tie, jacket and identity card, and cast off. The Grand Canal is the only sewer in the world which treats the sauntering passer-by to an experience as drunken as weighing anchor in the Marquesas.

Putting palaces on the beach is very like Alphonse Allais' conceit about the town in the country, except that this one works: the air really does seem purer there.

POOR AEDILES! Urban exodus, *acqua alta*, underground water table, tidal barrage and all the rest: these challenges are as nothing compared to their global responsibilities. We ask them to administer not only our Byzantine ceilings and our cravings for *morbidezza*, but also our latest International, the fifth of that name (and more flourishing than Leon Trotsky's Fourth), for which the domes of San Marco comprise a sort of Kremlin: the Mirror International. "Narcissists of all lands, unite! And do come and lean over the lagoon: shimmering reflections, so flattering." Not the lightest of tasks, managing the self-care of Western elites; and destined to grow heavier. Keeping the shimmer afloat and modernising it unceasingly. Like honour for nobles or virtue for republicans, narcissism is the ultimate cement for campanile enthusiasts. Their fundamental passion.

Islands in general are propitious for autism, for low-cost treats. In times gone by the narcissism of Rationality, philosophic and political, used to institute or invent distant Utopian islands, chess-board cities drawn with a ruler. The narcissism of the heart has appropriated this very temperate islet, where the waters are sweeter, the streets serpentine and the corners more rounded. So much less damaging.

Let us not forget a minor but relevant detail: water was the earliest reflecting surface experienced by the human species. Stagnant, oily and shining, it lends itself even better to private conversation. Like Venus and like the Image itself, Venice is *anadyomene*: all three are phantoms "born out of the foam" for our delectation, reflections slowly assembled by our desires over time. The cradle of our favourite painters and truest loves? Please: no tremolo. We are not there to enjoy Carpaccio or Titian or the face of our beloved—those are just glorious or tender pretexts—but to admire our own reflection. We go to Venice to talk, and be talked about. The place could never have fascinated generation after generation of featherless bipeds were it not supremely effective in making them regress to the mirror stage with its long, slow amazements: "Hey, yes, that's me, it really is me, look!" It gives everyone a licence to show off.

It is an established fact that a clouded, freckled glass inclines people to confession. Not a Calvinist examination of conscience or a resolute earnest examination of implications, but posthumous retrospection. "It is only now that my life is over that I return to contemplate myself in it," Morand begins his testamentary flashback. Self-flagellation is not the thing at all. Nor a laconic balance-sheet like Stendhal's. The undulating mirror inspires more tenderness than ferocity, more *sfumato* than exactitude. Erasing petty trivia like age and mistakes, the arcades of the Procuratie lengthen the outline like an evening shadow, rehabilitate a career through a classy disillusionment (the spent rake ennobled). A rite of early middle age for the high flyer or matter-of-fact senior manager, a Confucian test for the passage to the next rank: shedding a tear for his widowhoods ("I am Europe's widower"), his departed loves, his silted-up youth, then dashing it aside with a macho sweep of the back of his hand.

And it remains a good backdrop twenty years later for the stepping down, the lowering of the curtain, the farewells to the public, with sunset or moonlight (stick to the first). Just the sight of Fortune on her golden globe or the stone lions at the Arsenal makes Chateaubriand's goose-quill spring into existence between thumb and forefinger ("There is Venice, seated on the seashore like a beautiful woman who is going to die at dawn: the evening breeze lifts her scented hair; she is dying, saluted by all the graces and all the smiles of nature . . ."). Why should it be that Joseph Prudhomme[10] is more exposed than other men to this miraculous form of possession? Every year sees the appearance in the Paris bookshops of two or three unpublished chapters of *Memoirs from Beyond the Grave* which, printed under a pseudonym and with the slant if not the bearing of the viscount, are greeted with cries of rapture on every side.

I hope I will be forgiven for mentioning at this point the delicate, sometimes cruel dilemma in which the contemporary writer finds himself on the threshold of composition, but in these transparent times the public has a right to know something of the horrors that afflict the professionals who serve it with such self-denial. Two registers are available to the honest individual (the range being somewhat narrower than people imagine): madrigal and epitaph. Which should he give up? Should he play the dry classicist or the wet romantic? The eighteenth-century epicurean: a Laclos-like tone, witty, insolent, divine Marquis, candlelit supper, elegant offhand champagne; Casanova, Des Brosses, Bernis, with a dash of Nietzsche for profundity's sake? Or the suffering tone, consumptive, exhausted nostalgia, laboured languor; Barres, D'Annunzio, Noailles or Aschenbach? Watteau or Klimt? Mozart or Schumann? Two respirations, two prosodies. Double or quits.

Wiseacres cheat and try to play on both boards, spondee and dactyl. They still dream of combining partying in Venice with death in Venice, the light of chandeliers flickering on nacreous bosoms (three in the morning all the year round) with the purple agony of the sun setting San Giorgio ablaze (eight in the evening during September). The opportunist mixture unravels as it goes along, before your very eyes, but given what passes against this sort of background the customer is a good audience. It works, more or less. In the fiction business as in the Memoirs industry, Venice serves the author as a "completion bond" (as they call it in film production). Anyone who sets his little concoction in the triangle between the Florian, San Giorgio and the Záttere is playing on velvet. A guaranteed win (with the possible exception of thrillers, owing to the damped, softened, inexorable femininity of an atmosphere not especially appropriate to army Colt .45s or virile rough-and-tumble). It isn't difficult to understand the scrum of would-be tenants in the area around the Dogana: film-makers, novelists, painters and memorialists (philosophers are less at risk from best-sellers, therefore less in evidence).

We will set aside Gianfranco de Bosio's little-known masterpiece *Il terrorista*, a cold and serious film on the Italian Resistance in which gondolier folklore turns into *cinéma vérité* (as in Visconti's work, sumptuous décor combines in inverse fashion with a certain interior aridity).

If our guild had a deontology (to temper its essentially demagogic spirit), literary and film critics would have to agree on a principled penal system uniformly applicable to international products using Venice as a backdrop, like the one applied to films using children under twelve for tear-jerking purposes. Some sort of handicap is needed to offset the advantage mechanically conferred by these practices on those using them.

I OBSERVE an old German like a Grosz cartoon—frigid eye, hard profile, corseted torso—sitting at the front of the *vaporetto*, absorbed, transfigured, contemplating the rosettes and cornices of the *palazzi* gliding past. The old Jünger is radiating intense joy and taking deep breaths. I imagine him fifty years younger, uniformed and wearing a monocle. Yet another ex saved by golden mosaic, purified by the pink bubble. I watch him relax, smile, I see his eye suffuse with a sort of gentle candour. Cocooning, mothering, optical massage: an open-air aesthetotherapy session. A promising result. Back to Munich washed clean.

LA SALUTE: a fortunate metonymy. The whole of Venice has become a source of well-being, the ultimate sanctification of the secular. The disuse of its places of worship and the agnosticism of the professional Venetian do not invalidate this ethnological observation: the religiosity of the attitudes, ideas and language currently used by the aestheticising tribe. While ostentatiously scorning superstition, the disillusioned individual beyond good and evil, the dancing dandy, nevertheless invokes when necessary—so deep is piety's horror of the void—the spirit of seriousness associated with doctors of Beauty (André Gide: "a work of art is achieved only with the most virtuous elements of the mind"). Booted out of the door, the dog-collar clambers back in through the rose-window. Theatre of an initiatory form of worship, the *piazzetta* cannot help being edifying, exemplary, a lesson in deportment for the use of younger generations.

The Venice idiot is a penitent; the pilgrim of the Rare comes to the lagoon to cleanse his soul, to recover from his zoological misery. Apart from a sensual and falsely sensitive felicity, he seeks among the pigeons and pinnacles the justification of his existence, his redemption. A visit worthy of the name is not gratification but consecration of the custom of feasting to repletion once a year. Both material recompense for a hard year of toil and spiritual dedication to the god Art, to taste the host and the wine of beauty. This one week gives me the right to my small "share of eternity".

The symbolic power of this Mardi Gras. The miracle works on all the common run of men, if only they are also men of faith: Venice has the virtue of transsubstantiating (during a few nights in a hotel), not a disc of wafer into the flesh of the Lord but the manager, the currency trader, into a Pre-Raphaelite martyr. The lagoon doesn't just shelter us, it absolves us of our everyday nastinesses. A lustral bath, a philistine's stoop of holy water, in which Céline (that miscreant) spotted a variant of redemptive love, defined as "the infinite brought within the reach of poodles".

Switzerland washes whiter, but Venice washes pinker. The real laundry of the West, which is aesthetic, raises our jobberies into arias, our bodily filth into gilded crepuscular haze. This function gives the Venetian aura (in the northern hemisphere, above the $10,000 per capita threshold) an aspect that is genuinely religious, in the crudely Marxist sense of the word. One might thus envisage Venice as the opium of the rich, the *rentier*'s odour of sanctity, the aureole of our vale of tears, the soul of a soulless world, the point of honour of affairism, its solemn complement and its consolation, the longed-for refuge of poor creatures alienated by Footsie, CAC 40 and Dow Jones. What would become of us without this sheltering value of the immaterial, so welcoming to materialists, to the big game who roam stock exchange and forum? We can see with what kind of sacrality our mercantile society—all the more Venetian at weekends for being so money-grubbing during the week—has invested the Logetta and the Moorish quarterjacks on the Clock. In the Fifteenth Century the spiritual power of the Church was underpinned by the accumulation of temporal riches: plate and jewels, lands and prebends. In the Twentieth, the temporal powers of Capital are underwritten by the Grand Canal.

The Venice-Zurich axis was made official in 1991 at a World Arts Summit convened by the World Economic Forum, better known as the Davos group. Meeting in Venice, the elite of international business decided to meet its full responsibilities by supplying our official religion, Art, with the organ it lacked. The bankers resolved, according to their "Manifesto for a global society", to celebrate every four years in a "World arts village", with great pomp, not the supernatural marriage of the golden-horned Doge with the Adriatic (that obsolete piece of folklore from the time of the Bucentaur), but the more palpable wedding of the most important artists of the moment with "leaders from politics, business, media and science". The purpose of the conclave was to transcend "the diversity of cultures by creating a spirit of global unity" (*sic*). The central pivot of this new global spirituality, Venice, would serve as an ultimate hyphen between disunited civilisations. From imaginary museum to imaginary mysticism.

"SO WHERE ARE the doughty arsonists with blackened fingers? Let them come, let them belch flame along the library shelves! Blow up canals, flood museum basements! ... Ha! Let glorious canvases drift sodden in the scummy waves. Take picks and sledgehammers! Sap the foundations of venerable towns!" In the modernist candour, the "progressive" and avant-garde simplicity of their manifestos, the Italian Futurists made the mistake of condemning Venice for being fixated on the past.

Carrying a commonplace of the time to the point of stridency, the apostles of speed and the punch in the nose believed virtuously that the future ought to trample the past underfoot, that aeroplanes should obliterate antiquities and technology demolish superstition. Racing cars were going to smash the *Victory of Samothrace* under their speeding wheels! For the retrograde nature of progress had not yet become apparent to all. Since that time, we have learned that the new makes the archaic even more necessary, to our hearts as well as our societies; that the technological break acts as a spur to symbolic restoration everywhere, in the Midwest as well as Iran. However much of a substitute gadget it may be, the Venice pilgrimage has all the more future for being so ostentatiously retrograde. And not only because the "post-industrial civilisation" has an increasingly bulimic appetite for pre-industrial relics. There is more to it than that. The contemporary "crisis of representation"—what might be called for convenience "the death of theatre"—makes this holy place into a refuge of theatricality where we can catch our breath and refocus ourselves, so sated are we with happenings, so overloaded with data, so jangled by newsflashes and bewildered by immediate and uncontrollable presences. The clamour of live information, the aggressive worship of the primal, of the raw and exemplary, accentuate our need for rites and ceremonials, as well as for distance and orderly subdivision. The "society of spectacle", on the rocks everywhere else, survives in the venal enclave of a Fenice faced with nothing more threatening than full houses. Its basement may be foundering in slime and spilled crude, but an idealised Opera shimmers above the skyline of our frustrations.

Moreover, the use value of a town without wheels cannot help increasing with the multiplication of motorways, trucks, mopeds and jalopies. What I have called elsewhere the "jogging effect" of innovation— the less motorists have to walk the more they force themselves to run, driven by the threatened atrophy of their lower limbs—holds good in this case, on a world scale, for a sort of Venice effect of speed. "*Dans Venise la rouge, pas un bateau ne bouge*"? What a blessing, M. Musset, with the rest of the planet fidgeting all around it! A reassuring immobility, a still point at last. People speak of "losing themselves" in Venice; so let's go! Of course people play at losing themselves, but the fact is that wandering through this labyrinth really always means finding oneself: the pleasure of recognition, calm and free from vertigo. Slip under this portico again and check: everything is still in place, the lintel with its gargoyle, the little bar on the corner, the quadrilobate window . . . right down to the cats in the *campi*, still dozing in their usual places. In this century of disposable lighters and cameras, with the lifespan of objects growing shorter as that of human beings is lengthening, so ostentatious a permanence is beyond price. In the universal thirst for a return to the gondola, what moves us is the certainty of time retrieved: to be able to lean on a railing somewhere between Sant'Angelo and the Ca'Rezzonico, close our eyes and recite the grand succession of *palazzi*: Tito, Garzoni, Mocenigo, Contarini, Lezze . . . a labyrinth whose cadastral plan has not changed in five or six centuries, where Jean-Jacques Rousseau could find his way unaided tomorrow, turns the Baudelairean saw upside down: the heart of a mortal changes more rapidly, alas, than the shape of Venice. Doubtless that is the reason for this blessing· it is a place where people cry for themselves and not for the mutilated city, with its wormy and corroded piling.

Since slowness has become our most precious commodity, the ultimate criterion of civilisation, an islet where the pedestrian is king will never go unappreciated. Every stride there takes on a cinematic slow-motion quality, long shadows moving with the pompous stateliness of a prima donna or, when it is drizzling, a deep-sea diver. Indolence: treasure of the future. Better than idleness: exhausted feet at the end of every day, foot-ache as remedy for the pain of living. This guarantee of tiredness will always make the best of selling points for flabby-legged motorists and people in a hurry. Imagine Alitalia posters along the Los Angeles freeways: "Venice: the last place on earth where you have to walk . . . where you don't get to meetings on time".

But the tour operators will be lying if they promise the yuppies silence as well. With its streets like those hotel corridors that somehow broadcast vibrations through your pillow at night, its clicking footsteps and voices raised in drink, its landing-stages and growling motor launches, this earless village makes nearly as much clamour as a gridlocked city.

Is VENICE a mirror? Perhaps, but reflecting a fairly plausible future, welcome and pleasing . . . for it is the futurism of the catafalque, glimpsed or perhaps hallucinated, that people find frightening. Who could swear to its anachronism? It seems to me that the relic is not sufficiently out of fashion to take a holiday; the graceful, the delightful carries too much weight. Perhaps this egocentric microcosm, which

has always been a few centuries ahead of the rest—
which invented the ghetto long before the camps,
a department for monitoring correspondence long
before telephone tapping and the letter of credit long
before cashflow—is in the process of inventing before
our unseeing eyes the insular Europe of tomorrow,
reduced to picturesque features like half-timbering,
wrought iron and inns but dead to space exploration,
the planet and its century: a monocultural peninsula
set in its lagoon, forgetting the open sea, suffocated
by memory, and in which the tertiary sector will have
eclipsed the primary and secondary (Venice, too, in
the time of its supremacy, lived on the income from
its lands and industries). The memory-store of a
century hence, preserved in its reliquaries, painting
and polishing its decorative details, organising
commemorations: centenaries of this, millenaries of
that. A Paris inhabited by dotards, invaded by active
people from all over the world, gradually losing its
occupants (Venice sheds three a day), choked with
sediment, collapsing under the weight of guano,
given over to luxury manufacture, the hotel trade
and conservation; an antiquarian Paris with twice
as many tourists as Parisians, serenely savouring
the peace of museums and discussions, vituperating
the sacrilege of changes, clinging grimly to its last

function: that of labelling and homologating the art commodity, deeming "fit for exhibition" this or that uncertain, possibly vulgar novelty from far off (just as a few decades ago the Biennale enthroned Rauschenberg and pop art, awarding American art its long-awaited certificate of respectability). This storehouse of classified monuments, this "haven of beauty", would be the "dream refuge" of the Asia-Pacific zone, undervalued by the natives but symbolically overvalued by outsiders; the Pacific Basin might decide, in its infinite generosity, to add Europe to its inventory and turn it into the Venice of OAPEC. Symposiums of experts will meet in Seoul and Beijing to study corrosive soot and the pollution of the Seine, while technicians from Acapulco and Vancouver look into stone-rot in the Greater Louvre, and devise strategies for curbing the squatter pigeons of Westminster Abbey. Save Paris! Rescue packages for London, for Barcelona, for Amsterdam! Others meanwhile would anxiously be extrapolating demographic curves. Population of the historic centre of Venice, 1951: 191,000; 1966: 135,000; 1995: 70,000. But what does that matter? There are still 392 palaces, 105 churches and 22 convents.

The last defence of egotism, the reluctance to look at oneself in that way, to end up like that oneself. The refusal to catalogue oneself to death. The refusal to see my own group allowing itself to be poeticised, turned into "heritage", pickled in formaldehyde, numbered down to the last detail and yielded up to connoisseurs of glossy paper, Fortuny fabrics, Dresden china pug-dogs and Renaissance chimneypieces. I don't want a three-cornered carnival hat or lace cap to be slapped on my country's head. I don't want people to come and sprawl in the sun on my doorstep, their minds free and at ease. I don't want my portrait to be drawn, I don't want my nearest and dearest to be aestheticised. It is still too soon, in my opinion, to become Rialto, escutcheon, source of marbles and art of living, status symbol for collectors from Atlanta or gourmets from Kuala Lumpur.

I seem to remember that in the period of its greatness—for Venice was great—the iron-willed "triumphant City" was not loved. When it still had military strength and rights of veto, in the Lepanto era, nobody praised its mysterious grace or its cats slumbering between embroidered cushions. Its power—nuclear, industrious, restless and confrontational—was feared, not contemplated. "Sweet and magical clarity" is a thin recompense for inventing a world.

One has one's dignity, after all. This boudoir

illustrates the humiliation of our probable future. I cannot enjoy the spectacle of its shams, its afflictions, its decrepitudes: it is as if they were secretly our own. Collusion, premonition. Pocket mirror. Private shame. Yet another reason to draw a line through what some hospitals call the etiquette of compassion.

I AM ONLY too aware that I am being irritating. So why say anything in the first place? On these delicate and touchy subjects, too linked to the intimate, it would be better to yield the platform to men of influence, people of substance. I find it quite difficult enough to influence myself. So I will leave it at that. All the reasons in the world, good and bad, are ultimately powerless against the dictates of the heart. Listen: I can hear you—I can hear *us*—from here, already. Unstoppably.

"Of course, I know all that . . . but it's still *Venice*, isn't it?"

AFTERWORD

I DON'T KNOW how it is in Britain, but in France the Venice "religion" is first and foremost a mark of social distinction, a logo (so to speak) signalling to the common herd the existence of an aristocracy of taste. Outsnobbing snobs is a rather facile pleasure, hard to resist, to which I have yielded here by trying to show what is most vulgar, in the sense of inauthentic and artificial, about the devotees' pilgrimage. The epigram alone is insufficient, however. English-speaking readers should understand that the Venice referred to in this satire is just a metaphor, a sort of scapegoat. You could call it one symptom among others, made of eroded stone and stagnant waters. My quarrel is not with the picturesque city itself, but with the cult of worship that our elites have dedicated to it, their literary liturgies, their production-line adoration. In my mind the whole conceit was obvious, but the scandalised reactions of lagoon-lovers—not to mention la Serenissima's very thin-skinned aediles—soon persuaded me that what goes without saying is even better said. We should not confuse the thing with its function, or the urban idol with its idolaters' malpractices. Venice is no more responsible for its tourists than God is for his terrorists.

And as for the function, what is it? To serve as our consolation prize, as an excuse and recompense for the flatness of our lives, our pursuit of money, the standardisation of our responses. Visiting Venice is a Pharisee's Sabbath, the spiritual equivalent of sucking pebbles to assuage hunger in a materialism that uses guaranteed ecstasy to compensate for its deficit of meaning. A visit to Naples is a plunge into adventure (or at least it used to be, for that jungle-like city has also been heavily museumised over the last ten years or so). To visit Venice is to play safe. In order to forget or evade the pain involved in the production of meaning or beauty, the whims and excesses of aesthetic passion (the collector's as well as the creator's), we fall back on a pre-packaged, labelled beauty, smug and motionless.

An underlying purpose of this lampoon, behind the museum-town, was to exorcise the looming spectre of a wholly museumised Europe. Of an Old World running out of steam, no longer an actor but a mere spectator in its own destiny, memorialising its exit from history with a fussy sacralisation of dead and embalmed forms. Might not the inflation of "heritage", the growing craze for antiques and relics, the cult of monuments, of commemoration and quotation, conceal some sort of funereal vertigo, a lascivious dwelling on the void? Beauty vitrified, touched up, reduced to a mythical version of itself, to an end in itself, in those social parades that our cities of art have become: is not this narcissistic and macabre joy, redolent of Alexandrine periods and dying cultures? Of course the postcard version of Venice is not a cause but an effect, and to attribute the vices of its worshippers to the totem itself would be fetishism in reverse. One could go on for ever about what is called the end of a civilisation. But that would be another sort of literature, more academic and fastidious. For the present text I have preferred summary to dissertation and a light-hearted tone to the accents of elegy. For that I apologise.

RÉGIS DEBRAY, Paris, 8 December 2001

NOTES

1. M. Homais, a character in *Madame Bovary*, personifies bourgeois fatuousness.
2. François Coppée (1842–1908), French poet, author of lyrics depicting lives of the poor.
3. Constantin Guys (1802–1892), French draughtsman and watercolourist, admired by Baudelaire who described him as "the painter of modern life".
4. Giorgio de Chirico (1888–1978), Italian painter, born in Greece, founder of surrealist movement who later reverted to more classical style.
5. Carlo Goldoni (1707–1793), Venetian comic playwright.
6. La république Parthénopéenne, a short-lived republic founded in Naples by Napoleon in 1799.
7. A porous stone composed of compacted volcanic ash and other ejected material.
8. Sulpicien: member of the Compagnie des prêtres de Saint-Sulpice, a society formed by the *curé* of the church of that name in Paris, along with an eponymous seminary, for the training of priests. The religious images sold in the neighbourhood were in notably bad taste.
9. A wooden image (like a "dimestore Indian") of a Chinese in the Florian café in St Mark's Square. But also refers to Paul Morand, right-wing French writer and Venice fanatic, who looked Chinese.
10. Inept and sententious petit-bourgeois character invented by Henri Monnier (1799–1877), French writer and caricaturist.

PUSHKIN PRESS

Pushkin Press was founded in 1997. Having first rediscovered European classics of the twentieth century, Pushkin now publishes novels, essays, memoirs, children's books, and everything from timeless classics to the urgent and contemporary.

This book is part of the Pushkin Collection of paperbacks, designed to be as satisfying as possible to hold and to enjoy. It is typeset in Monotype Baskerville, based on the transitional English serif typeface designed in the mid-eighteenth century by John Baskerville. It was litho-printed on Munken Premium White Paper and notch-bound by the independently owned printer TJ International in Padstow, Cornwall. The cover, with French flaps, was printed on Colorplan Pristine White paper. The paper and cover board are both acid-free and Forest Stewardship Council (FSC) certified.

Pushkin Press publishes the best writing from around the world—great stories, beautifully produced, to be read and read again.